Mikaela Shiffrin

by Grace Hansen

OLYMPIC BIOGRAPHIES

Abdo Kids Jumbo is an Imprint of Abdo Kids
abdopublishing.com

abdopublishing.com

Published by Abdo Kids, a division of ABDO, P.O. Box 398166, Minneapolis, Minnesota 55439.
Copyright © 2019 by Abdo Consulting Group, Inc. International copyrights reserved in all countries.
No part of this book may be reproduced in any form without written permission from the publisher.
Abdo Kids Jumbo™ is a trademark and logo of Abdo Kids.

052018

092018

Photo Credits: AP Images, Getty Images, iStock, Shutterstock

Production Contributors: Teddy Borth, Jennie Forsberg, Grace Hansen

Design Contributors: Dorothy Toth, Laura Mitchell

Library of Congress Control Number: 2018936110

Publisher's Cataloging in Publication Data

Names: Hansen, Grace, author.

Title: Mikaela Shiffrin / by Grace Hansen.

Description: Minneapolis, Minnesota : Abdo Kids, 2019 | Series: Olympic
    biographies set 2 | Includes glossary, index and online resources (page 24).

Identifiers: ISBN 9781532181443 (lib. bdg.) | ISBN 9781532181542 (ebook) |
    ISBN 9781532181597 (Read-to-me ebook)

Subjects: LCSH: Shiffrin, Mikaela--Juvenile literature. | Olympic athletes--Juvenile literature. |

Winter Olympics--Juvenile literature. | Alpine skiing--Juvenile literature.

Classification: DDC 796.93092 [B]--dc23

Table of Contents

Early Years

Mikaela Shiffrin was born on

March 3, 1995 in Vail, Colorado.

Vail

5

Mikaela's parents were good skiers. They taught Mikaela to ski in their driveway at the age of 2.

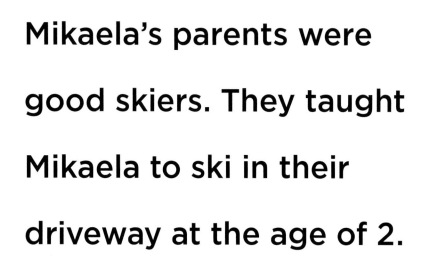

In 2003, Mikaela moved to New Hampshire with her family. There, she worked hard on her skills. She did not race as much as other skiers. Instead, she focused mainly on **drills**.

8

9

Competing

In the 2012-13 World Cup

season, Mikaela won three

slalom events!

10

11

She went on to win her

first gold at the 2013

World Championships.

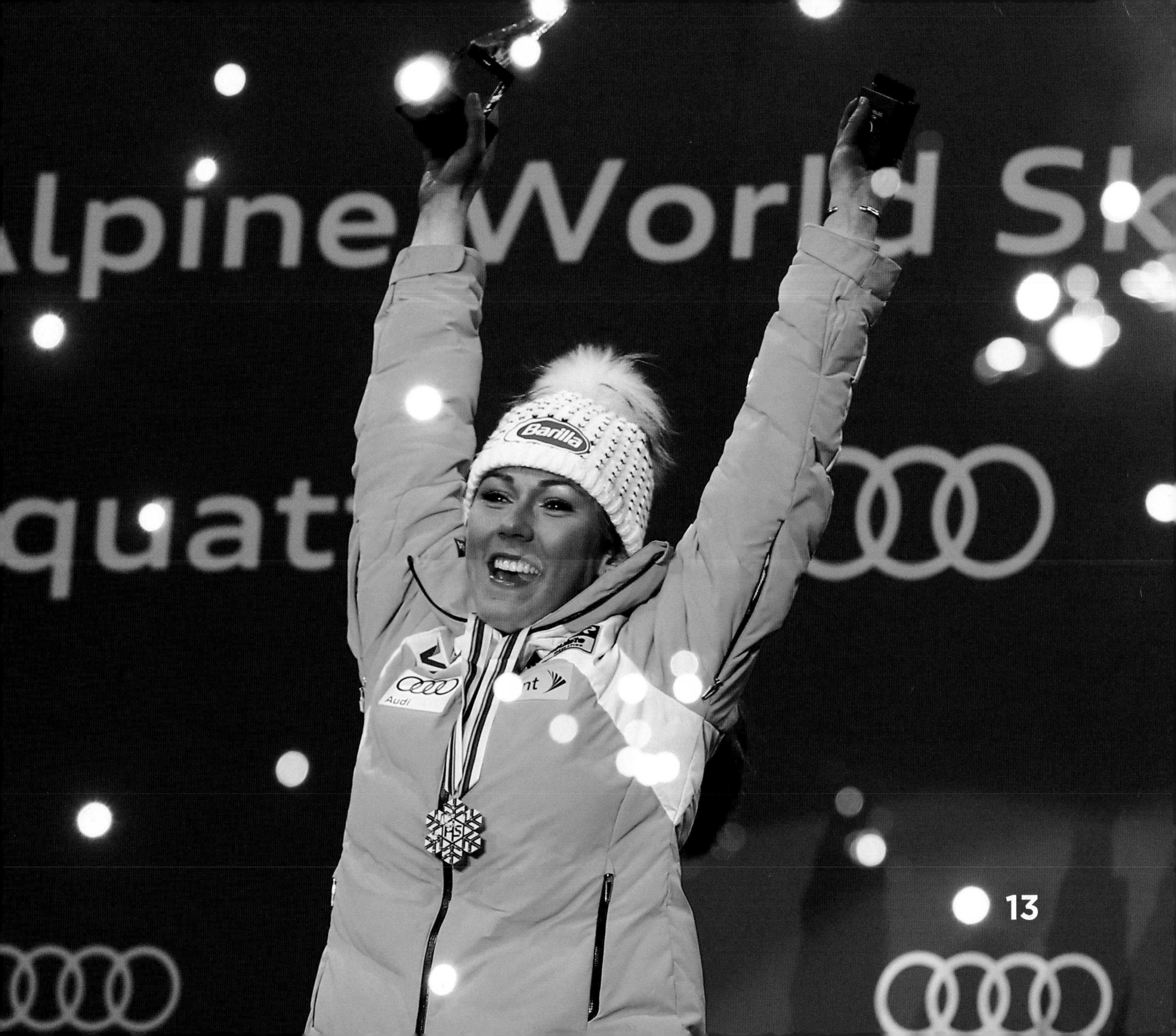
World
Barilla
Audi

Sochi

The Sochi Winter Olympics were in 2014. Mikaela won gold in the women's **slalom**! At 18, she was the youngest Olympian to win the event.

14

First & Gold

In the 2017-18 World Cup
season, Mikaela placed first 11
times. This brought her World
Cup wins to 42!

Mikaela joined team USA again at the 2018 Winter Olympics in South Korea. She won gold in the **giant slalom** event!

19

Mikaela won silver in the combined event. She was proud of herself after the Olympics. She said that with moments of victory and defeat, "I'm walking away with a huge smile."

More Facts

- Mikaela has the letters "ASFTTB" on her helmet. It stands for "Always ski faster than the boys."

- Mikaela brought 35 pairs of skis to the Olympics. However, she often travels with 70 pairs. This is because she regularly competes in all five Alpine events.

- The skis are ready for their certain event and for certain snow conditions. They are different lengths and have different amounts of wax on them. They can also be made from different materials.

Glossary

drill – a repetitive training exercise to get better at something.

giant slalom – an event where a skier races down a winding course marked by flags or poles that are placed farther from each other than in the slalom event.

slalom – an event where a skier races down a winding course marked by flags or poles.

Index

Abdo Kids
ONLINE
FREE! ONLINE MULTIMEDIA RESOURCES

Visit **abdokids.com** and
use this code to access crafts,
games, videos, and more!

Abdo Kids Code:
OMK1443

24